The Grateful Gazelle

Written by:
Jemma Ward

Illustrated by:
Eve Morgan

Published in association with
Bear With Us Productions

© 2024 Jemma Ward
The Grateful Gazelle

ISBN: 978-1-3999-9092-9

Cover by Richie Evans
Design by Tommaso Pigliapochi
Illustrated by Eve Morgan

www.justbearwithus.com

The Grateful Gazelle
Written by:
Jemma Ward

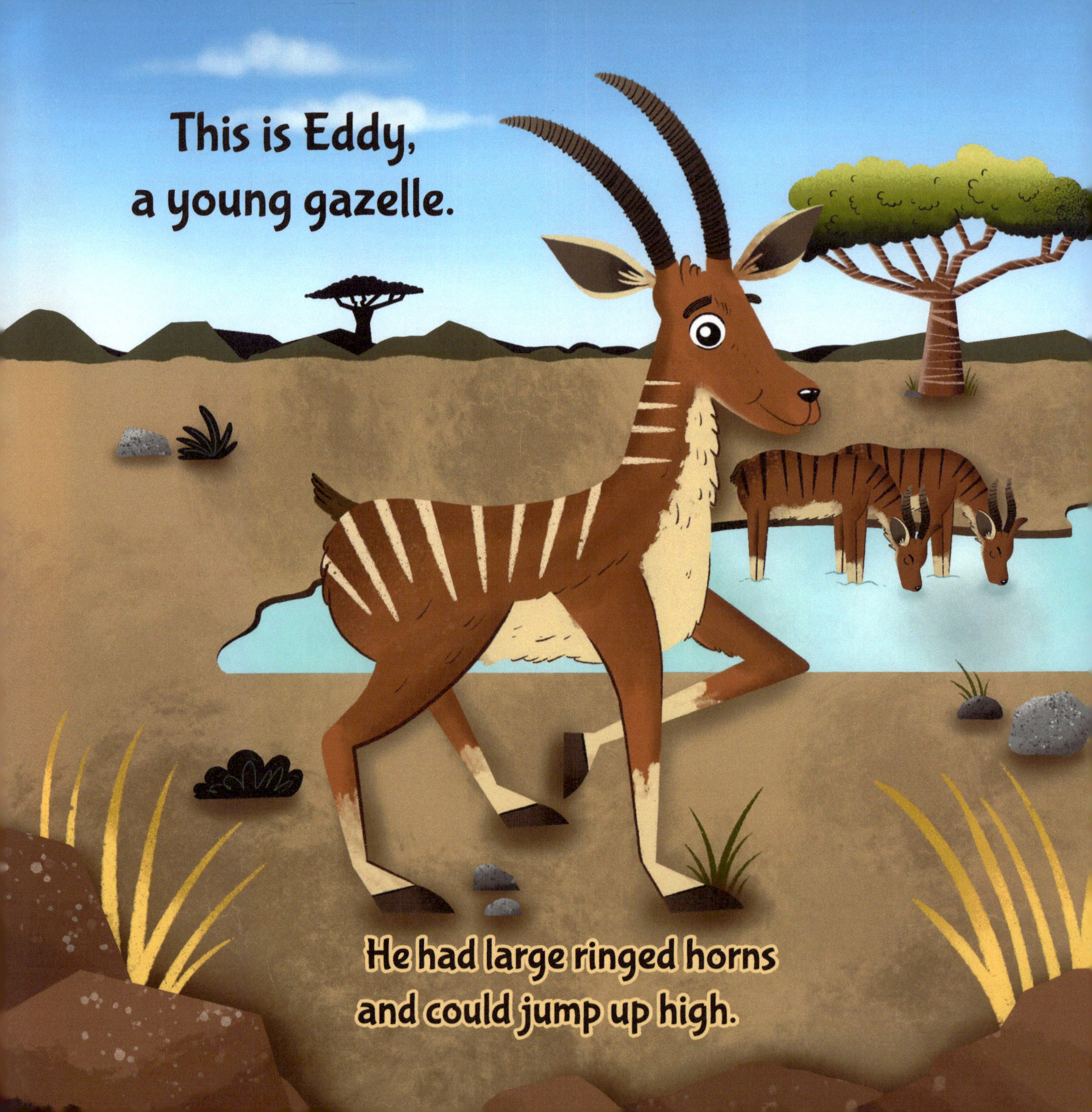

This is Eddy,
a young gazelle.
He had large ringed horns
and could jump up high.

Eddy Gazelle was beautiful and could be as fast as a cheetah by leaping in the sky.

Eddy was bright and curious; he loved to explore. His heart was full of joy, but he had a dream to find something more.

He would gaze at the elephants, giraffes, and monkeys across the way. Longing to be friends with the other animals to dance and to play.

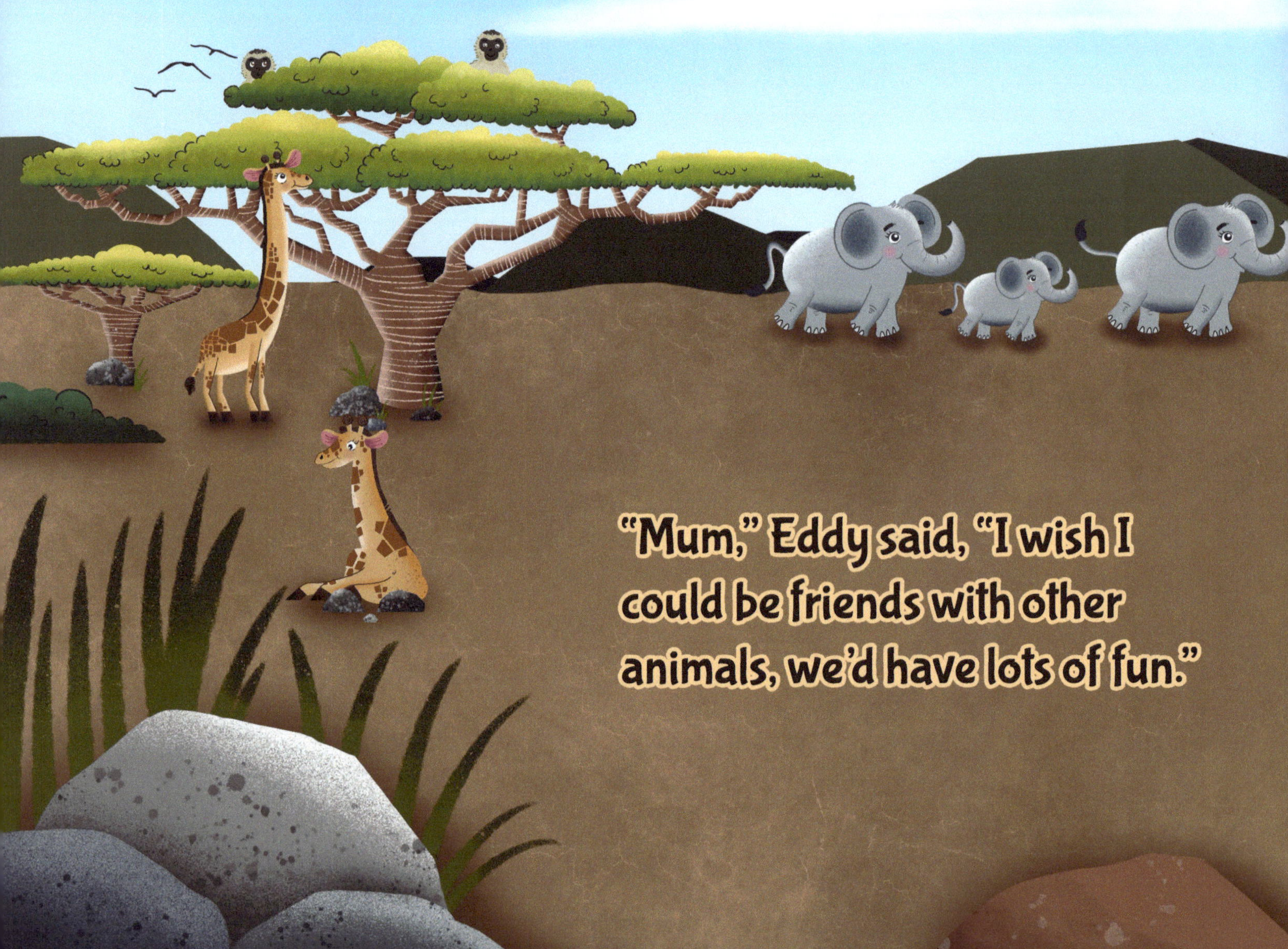

His mum replied gently, "You know we don't mix;
we stay in our herds, that's how it's done."

Although he had a wish, Eddy was grateful for what he had and felt complete.

One day Eddy awoke.
He smiled and joyfully jumped to his feet.

He trotted through the bushes,
singing and prancing along,

Looking around hoping to make friends,
maybe his mum was wrong.

As Eddy strolled further,
he heard a funny sound.
Curiously, he slowly moved his
hooves on the ground.

It seemed to be
coming from
behind that tree.

"Hello," he said softly, "don't
be shy, my name is Eddy."

Eddy watched as leaves moved, there was rustling and a grunt. To his amazement stepped out a beautiful small grey elephant.

She had big floppy ears, a long grey trunk and wide feet.
Eddy was delighted, a new friend he could now meet!

Eddy said, "Hi there, friend, what is your name? I am on an adventure, are you doing the same?" The little elephant was frightened and hid behind her ears. She said her name was Lola as she began to fully appear.

"Don't be scared," Eddy said, "be grateful for what you can see. Being grateful is the best way to help you to be happy." Eddy was kind and looked for ways to help others. Lola was delighted as she gazed around at the pretty colours.

"Come on, Lola, let's go on an adventure in search for some fruit. We can take it back to your herd, let's go down this route."

Strolling along, they heard a noise followed by a frightened scream. Looking up into the trees they saw a monkey clinging to a beam.

The monkey sniffled. "I was swinging, holding my bananas, but they did fall." "We'll help, we're already on an adventure for fruit, bananas and all."

The monkey, called Beans,
relaxed and began to unfold.
Eddy said, "This will be fun;
the bananas can be our gold!

I think we will find your
bananas and so much more."
Lola added, "Yes, as we walk
together, we get to explore!"

Believing they would find the fruit, Eddy thought,
How lucky we are! Now we have new friends,
even though us animals usually stay afar!

The three new friends travelled along,
Finding many wonderous creatures,
colours and songs.

They skipped and laughed, having lots of fun. Until Lola bumped into something and fell on her bum. "Ouch," Lola said, "I've bumped my head."

Then a voice came from above which curiously said, "Excuse me, who is that down below?" Eddy looked up and shouted, "Hello!"

Lola added, "My name is Lola, I'm sorry I did not see you there."

The three friends looked up to see a giraffe with a gentle glare.

"It's alright," the giraffe replied.
"I am indeed just fine."
Happy, Eddy smiled and his
eyes they did shine.

The giraffe said, "My name is Zuri. Here, please take these flowers. My family is over there. Did you know as a group we are called towers?"

The friends looked at the giraffes nearby – so beautiful and high.

They were fascinating and some of them even touched the sky.

"Wow," Eddy said as his face lit up,
"this really is a special day.
It's nice to meet you all, would you
like to come and play?

We are on an
adventure looking
for lost gold."

"That sounds fun!"
And their adventure
continued to unfold.

At last they found the gold
shining as brightly as can be.
Beans grabbed the bananas,
but there was something more
they could see.

"This tree looks special,"
Zuri said, "let me get
a better look."

She stretched her neck
high pushing the leaves
as the tree shook.

The tree was a scrummy fig tree, with figs that were ripe and ready to eat.
Beans and Lola could not believe it, these were elephants' and monkeys' favorite treat.

The friends gathered lots of figs, then went back to their herds,

And told them of their adventure and all that they had learnt.

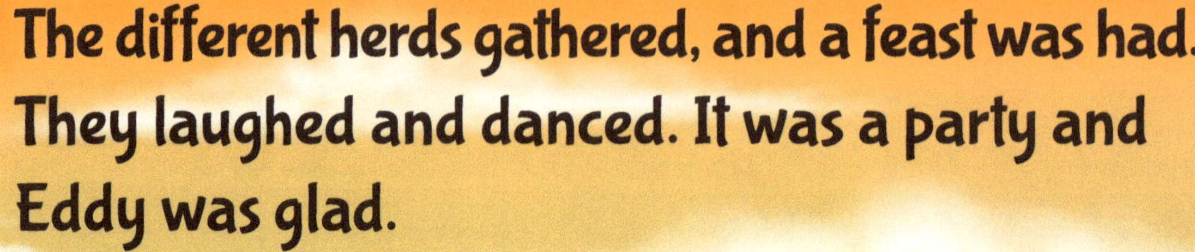

The different herds gathered, and a feast was had.
They laughed and danced. It was a party and
Eddy was glad.

"Mum," Eddy said, "dreams do come true;
you just have to believe. There is magic
around us if we stop to look and see."

All was good – Eddy's
dream had come true,
He would have more
adventures – with his new–
found friends too.